Picture a Sunset

Written by Teresa Heapy

Illustrated by Paddy Donnelly

RISING ★ STARS

Do you know what a sunset is?

day

sunrise

A sunset happens when the day ends.

sunset

night

A sunset can turn the sky lots of different colours.

Some parts of the sky are light.
Some parts are dark.

Can you make a sunset picture?

Look at a photograph to start.

Can you see:

land	yellow
Sun	gold
clouds	lilac
sky	blue
	orange
	pink

Make your sunset picture

You will need:

paper
pencil
rubber
glitter
paint

Pick some little things to add to your picture too!

1. Draw your sunset picture in pencil.

paper

rubber

Rub out any bits that are not right!

2. Paint your picture. Use lots of different colours.

Wash your brush between paint colours!

3. Brush glue on the paper.

4. Stick things on.

5. Let it dry.

6. Use glitter to show the light.

Dab on glue.

Tap glitter on top.

Tip it off!

What a fantastic sunset picture
that is!

Look for the sunset when the day ends.
What colours will you see?

Talk about the book

Ask your child these questions:

1 When does a sunset happen?

2 What materials do you need to make a sunset picture?

3 Why would you look at a photograph to start?

4 Why should you wash your brush between paint colours?

5 Can you explain how to make a sunset picture?

6 Have you ever seen the Sun set over the sea? What did it look like?